CODING CAREERS
IN TRANSPORTATION

Jeri Freedman

Cavendish
Square

New York

Published in 2020 by Cavendish Square Publishing, LLC
243 5th Avenue, Suite 136, New York, NY 10016

Library of Congress Cataloging-in-Publication Data

Names: Freedman, Jeri, author.
Title: Coding careers in transportation / Jeri Freedman.
Description: First edition. | New York, NY : Cavendish Square Publishing,
LLC, 2020. | Series: Coding careers for tomorrow | Includes bibliographical references and index.
Identifiers: LCCN 2019004132 (print) | LCCN 2019005241 (ebook) |
ISBN 9781502645920 (ebook) | ISBN 9781502645913 (library bound) | ISBN 9781502645906 (pbk.)
Subjects: LCSH: Transportation engineering–Data processing–Vocational guidance–
Juvenile literature. Classification: LCC TA1160 (ebook) | LCC TA1160 .F74 2020 (print) |
DDC 629.040285/51–dc23 LC record available at https://lccn.loc.gov/2019004132

Editorial Director: David McNamara
Editor: Kristen Susienka
Copy Editor: Denise Larrabee
Associate Art Director: Alan Sliwinski
Designer: Ginny Kemmerer
Production Coordinator: Karol Szymczuk
Photo Research: J8 Media

The photographs in this book are used by permission and through the courtesy of: Cover LPette/
iStock/Getty Images, background (and used throughout the book) Maciek905/iStockphoto.
com; p. 4 Johnny H5/iStock/Getty Images; p. 6 Angelo Giampiccolo/Shutterstock.com; p. 8
Popperfoto/Getty Images,background (and used throughout the book) MF3d/iStockphoto.
com; p. 11 Randy Duchaine/Alamy Stock Photo; p. 12 Daniel Karmann/Picture Alliance/Getty
Images; p. 14 Avigator Thailand/Shutterstock.com; p. 21 SeongJoon Cho/Bloomberg/Getty
Images; p. 22 Eppic Photography/iStockphoto.com; p. 24, 28 John Greim/LightRocket/
Getty Images; p. 32 Smith Collection/Gado/Getty Images; p. 34 Metamorworks/iStock/Getty
Images; p. 37 Chesky/Shutterstock.com; p. 42 Vadim Rodnev/Shutterstock.com; p. 44 Courtesy
Rolls-Royce; p. 46 Francois Nascimbeni/AFP/Getty Images; p. 50 Jason Alden/Bloomberg/
Getty Images; p. 52 NC Collections/Alamy Stock Photo; p. 54 Tony Avelar/AP Images; p.
57 FatCamera/E+/Getty Images; p. 60 fstop123/iStock/Getty Images; p. 64 Asiee/E+/Getty
Images; p. 66 Eric Seals/TNS/Newscom; p. 70 David Paul Morris/Bloomberg/Getty Images.

Printed in the United States of America

Contents

Controlling congestion on highways requires new electronic technologies. This traffic jam is in Los Angeles, California.

chapter_01

The Transportation Industry

For decades, computerization has played a role in the planning of logistics (the movements of goods), the designing of highways and vehicles, and the automation of all methods of transportation. In the twenty-first century, research and development for the automation of both transportation systems and vehicles have increased, and the opportunities for coders in the transportation industry have grown as well.

TRANSPORTATION SYSTEMS

The transportation system includes all infrastructure that makes movement from one place to another possible, such as highways, railroads, airports, and shipping lanes. For the majority of people, the most familiar part of the transportation network is the highway system. At one time, highways were simply networks of paved roads, traffic lights were only automated to change at timed intervals, and toll booths were literally stalls in which a human attendant collected money to allow vehicles to pass. Increasingly, however, computer hardware and software are being used to make the entire highway system smarter, creating a need for programmers.

It is not just highways that are becoming smarter. Systems throughout the transportation infrastructure (basic systems and structures) continue to advance, requiring new programs for monitoring and control. Among such applications are the following:

This air traffic controller in Italy monitors the position of planes on a radar system.

Air traffic control: The Federal Aviation Administration (FAA) has implemented a project to combine automated systems with human air traffic controllers for managing aircraft in flight. Both the National Aeronautics and Space Administration (NASA) and the US Air Force are working on automated systems for controlling drones for domestic and military applications, respectively.

Train control: Systems that provide real-time information to train drivers are being implemented to improve the safety and operation of trains, as well as to optimize travel times and improve punctuality. Automated and "smart" control systems are under development that will reduce or eliminate the need for human intervention.

Subway control: New systems are being designed that provide functionality, ranging from trains on a line that can communicate their location automatically to each other to fully automated self-driving trains.

Traffic control: Systems have been implemented to use sensors embedded in the roads to adjust the timing of stoplights at various times of day, based on traffic flow. Smarter systems are being planned that would use roadside sensors to adjust the timing of stoplights in real time, and to provide information to drivers about conditions ahead on different routes.

Reginald Denny and the Mass-Produced Drone

This is a photograph of Reginald Denny, taken around 1921.

Unmanned autonomous vehicles (UAVs), better known as drones, have become common for both military and civilian use. Their origin goes back further than many people realize. Reginald Denny was an aircraft gunner in the British Royal Flying Corps during World War I. He created the first mass-produced UAV for military use. World War I ended in 1918, and shortly after, Denny moved to Hollywood. There he worked as an actor but also developed radio-controlled model aircraft throughout the 1930s. In 1934, along with business partners, he formed Reginald Denny Industries and opened the Reginald Denny Hobby Shop on Hollywood Boulevard, where he sold radio-controlled model planes. This business enterprise later became the Radioplane Company, which produced low-cost, radio-controlled drones used in training army antiaircraft gunners to shoot down planes.

Over time, Denny improved the drone. In 1940, the army gave him a small contract for the fourth version, the RP-4, renamed the OQ-1 Radioplane. The OQ designation indicated a scaled-down target. In 1941, the army placed a much larger order for the RP-5, dubbed the OQ-2. The US Navy bought the drone as well, renaming it Target Drone, Denny 1 (TDD-1). Radioplane ultimately built thousands of drones for the military during World War II. In 1952, the company was bought by the defense company Northrup.

As for Denny, he continued his acting career in movies and television. His last role was playing Commodore Schmidlapp in the 1966 film Batman. Denny's drones created an interest on the part of the military and a component of the defense industry that continues to this day.

Automated vehicles: Many companies are working on fully autonomous vehicles for business, consumer, and military use. Remote-controlled drones currently exist, but the goal is to create driverless, completely self-controlled planes, trains, buses, cars, trucks, and ships. The military is also pursuing completely autonomous drones and vehicles.

JOBS FOR CODERS IN THE TRANSPORTATION INDUSTRY

There are two aspects to the transportation industry. The first is the infrastructure that allows transportation to take place. This includes the physical roads, bridges, rails, airports, and similar facilities on which vehicles operate, and the systems that monitor and control traffic and vehicles. The second part of the transportation industry is the vehicles themselves. Traditionally, infrastructure has consisted of immovable structures made of materials such as concrete, steel, and asphalt. Control systems have been operated by human workers who make decisions based on information received through electric or electronic means. Most vehicles have been mechanical and operated by human drivers. Advances in technology have led to the development of sensors that can note changes in the operation of a component and alert a person if there is an issue, whether with a car engine or a moving train. However, this technology has been mostly limited to informing a human operator, who then takes action he or she deems appropriate.

This situation is changing, though. Both companies and regulatory agencies, such as the FAA and Department of Transportation (DOT), are designing and implementing new computerized transportation systems and vehicles. The goal is to make traveling safer, more efficient, and less costly. Smart highways, automated control systems for trains, planes, and public transportation, and autonomous vehicles for civilian and military use are being developed that will radically change the nature of transportation. Because much of the transportation infrastructure in the United States is old,

Control center employees at Grand Central Terminal in New York City track the movements of trains.

these changes mean creating new systems and writing very large amounts of code. Modernizing and automating the transportation system, and creating new types of vehicles, will provide opportunities for programmers for years to come.

Coders are needed in the transportation industry to perform many tasks. They write software to control autonomous vehicles. They provide code for systems that monitor remote sensors to track the location of vehicles such as trains, buses, and trucks. They create programs to run automated highway components such as stoplights, tollbooths, and streetlights. They work on the software for

A car drives over an expansion joint that contains sensors, part of a smart bridge in Nuremberg, Germany.

the new smart highway, air traffic, and public transportation control systems. In essence, they help operate the many systems that make our modern world function. While technologies may be advancing, there will continue to be a need for coders to program components and oversee the systems they create.

This aerial view shows an interchange on the Interstate Highway System.

chapter_02

Coding in the Transportation Industry

The availability and nature of transportation have shaped the development of countries and have played major roles in their physical and economic growth. Settlements, towns, and cities grew near waterways, roads, and later, highways. In the United States, trains—and later airplanes and truck routes—linked the densely populated coastal areas with the agricultural heartland of the interior. The automobile allowed for the development of suburbs as the middle class moved out of congested cities. Today, public transportation technology continues to evolve, constantly adopting new tools. Smart highways and autonomous vehicles are radically changing transportation.

A BRIEF HISTORY OF TRANSPORTATION

The economies of countries from earliest times until the eighteenth century were agricultural. Many people farmed and sold their crops for profit. However, technological advancements in the late eighteenth century changed the basic nature of societies from agricultural to industrial. The eighteenth century saw the development of steam engines to power machines. Coal-fired steam engines made steamships and railroads possible.

Steam technology also changed public transportation, which until the 1870s consisted of horse-drawn trolleys. In the 1880s and 1890s, the ability of coal-fired power plants to produce electricity allowed for the construction of cable cars and electric streetcars, which drew their power from wires strung along streets.

THE RISE OF THE AUTOMOBILE

No mode of transportation better captures the relationship between transportation and technology than the automobile. Leonardo da Vinci sketched the first design for a self-propelled vehicle around 1480. Da Vinci's "self-propelled cart" moved by means of coiled springs that were wound by rotating the tires (it operated similarly to windup toys that move across a floor). It could be steered by means of a rod attached to the front tire; brakes could be activated by pulling a rope. A practical version of da Vinci's design was not produced until 2004, when the Galileo Museum, Institute of the History of Science in Florence, Italy, constructed one—and found that it actually worked.

In the 1700s, several European inventors drew plans for vehicles designed to move by wind power, using mounted windmills or sails, while other researchers experimented with clockwork mechanisms. Advances continued throughout the decades. Once steam engines were invented at the end of the eighteenth and beginning of the nineteenth centuries, inventors started creating ways to produce steam-powered automobiles. Some inventors thought that electric vehicles would be easier to operate, but it wasn't possible to build them until a powerful electric storage battery could be invented. In 1859, Gaston Planté invented the electric storage battery in France. In 1881, Camille Alphonse Faure created an improved version, which made electric cars possible.

The end of the nineteenth century and the beginning of the twentieth century led to even more advances. In the 1880s, German inventors Karl Benz and Gottlieb Daimler independently created gasoline-powered cars, which used an internal combustion engine. This engine mixes fuel with air and burns it to produce energy. Charles and Frank Duryea created the first successful American gasoline-powered automobile between 1892 and 1893. The Ford Motor Company, headed by Henry Ford, started operation in 1903.

It revolutionized the automobile industry by mass-producing cars, using interchangeable parts and assembly lines. This process made it possible to produce more cars faster, and to sell them at a cheaper price, making them affordable for average people.

Beginning in 1916, the US government provided large amounts of funding for constructing and upgrading roads. However, most roads were built by local municipalities and had one or two lanes and many stoplights at intersections. In 1956, Congress enacted the Federal-Aid Highway Act, which created the Interstate Highway System, today a 46,876-mile (75,439-kilometer) network of high-speed highways that cross the country. This highway system—without stoplights and with under- and overpasses instead of intersections—was designed to allow higher-speed travel and reduce congestion.

In the 1970s, two factors created a renewed interest in electric cars. One was a fuel crisis caused by the limiting of oil output by the oil cartel OPEC, and the other was an increasing awareness of the negative effects on the environment by gasoline exhaust fumes. In response, a number of automotive manufacturers began developing electric vehicles, but such vehicles could only travel a limited distance before recharging, which restricted their desirability. In the next few decades, mainstream manufacturers turned to hybrid vehicles, which allowed drivers to switch to gas when electric power ran out. In 1997, car company Toyota introduced its electric Prius hybrid.

Demand was so high, there was a waiting list to get one. The success of the Prius demonstrated to other manufacturers that there was a demand for electric vehicles and caused other car companies to begin manufacturing them.

Today, advances in automotive technologies are still being proposed and tested. For example, luxury electric car company Tesla is attempting to create batteries that last longer. There has also been an increase in the number of charging stations available, which makes it easier to recharge electric vehicles.

As of 2018, a decrease in the price of gasoline due to securing oil from new sources, such as shale and oil sand fields, has reduced the cost of operating gasoline-powered cars. As a result, more people are driving large vehicles such as SUVs, which are too large and heavy to go far on existing battery technology. That is not to say that stronger batteries capable of operating these vehicles could never be possible. For now, however, it seems solely battery-operated automobiles are becoming less popular.

AUTOMATING AUTOMOBILES

Throughout the twentieth and twenty-first centuries, automobiles have become increasingly automated. Computerization of cars began in 1968, when Volkswagen started using a computer-controlled electronic fuel injection (EFI) system. In the 1970s, computer-controlled anti-skid braking systems and computer-controlled transmission systems were added to cars.

Today, there are more than fifty computerized systems for monitoring and controlling every aspect of operating a car, including engine functions, parking, lane monitoring, and communication. Numerous automakers and technology companies are working on autonomous vehicles, including Ford, GM, Tesla, Volkswagen, BMW, Lyft, Uber, and Google/ Alphabet (Waymo).

IT IN THE TRANSPORTATION INDUSTRY

People often think the terms "programmer" and "coder" mean the same thing, and they use them interchangeably. These words describe someone who writes instructions, called code, that cause a computer to perform a particular task. In some instances, the two words have different meanings. "Programmer" is used to describe someone who writes a software program from scratch, whereas "coder" means someone who uses a software program to create an application that performs a certain function—for example, using a data analysis program to retrieve information on traffic flows on a given stretch of highway at various times.

There are many job prospects for coders in the transportation industry. Increasing congestion and aging

These self-driving cars in South Korea are being run on a test track to evaluate their performance.

infrastructure mean that data analysts are needed to provide information to engineering firms for use in the development of new routes and expansion projects; to do research on transportation usage and trends for city, state, and federal governments and consulting and engineering firms; and to write code for smart highway and autonomous vehicle applications. The more advances the industry makes, the more need there is for people who can program and test new systems.

Transportation companies are making capital investments in computer hardware and software used for designing better highways, controlling existing vehicles, and creating

smart traffic systems

Smart traffic signals, like Surtrac, change in response to the actual traffic present.

Computer technology is changing the way that traffic is handled on roads and highways. The timers on traditional traffic lights only turn them on and off at set intervals, regardless of the time of day or level of traffic. Beginning in the 1980s, some cities started to improve on real-time traffic management by embedding sensors beneath the road in front of the signals to trigger a change in the signal when they sense vehicles. Today, highways are becoming smarter. Private companies, cities, states, and the US Department of Transportation are all exploring ways to optimize the flow of traffic. For example, the Robotics Institute and Traffic21 labs at Carnegie Mellon University in Pittsburgh, Pennsylvania, have developed a new approach to real-time traffic signal control. Their system, called Surtrac, uses artificial intelligence to coordinate the performance of traffic signals with the traffic that is actually on a road. Surtrac changes signals to produce the optimal traffic flows throughout a specified area, not just the one road. It can change the traffic arrangement in seconds, and it takes into account not just motor vehicle traffic but also bicyclists, pedestrians, and public transit such as buses and trolleys. When used in place of traditional traffic signal timing and earlier embedded sensor systems, Surtrac has reduced travel times by 25 percent, time spent waiting at signals by 40 percent, stops by 30 percent, and emissions by 20 percent.

automated vehicles. Coders create applications that ultimately lead to systems that have fewer disruptions and accidents, are more efficient, and cost less. Therefore, transportation companies and regulatory agencies such as the FAA and the Department of Transportation have come to see information technology as a vital tool. The adoption of advanced computer technology by transportation companies and agencies is radically changing the nature of transportation.

TECHNOLOGY FOR BETTER TRANSPORTATION

The major trend in all aspects of transportation is increasing automation—on land, at sea, and in the air. Air traffic control is

Air traffic control centers, like this one at Phildelphia International Airport, are adopting automation to improve efficiency.

one area that is being affected by the transition to automation. Traditionally, this function has been carried out by human beings stationed in control towers. They rely on Terminal Radar Approach Control (TRACON) to handle takeoff and landing control within a radius of 30 to 50 nautical miles (55 to 92 km) around an airport. Once an airplane gets beyond this distance, en route air traffic control centers take over control of the routing. As planes travel across the country, they switch from one en route air traffic control center to another (four to five of them for a route across the United States, for example). Air traffic controllers make routing decisions for planes in real time. The FAA is attempting to modernize and automate the air traffic control system through the En Route Automation Modernization program (ERAM), which was designed for the FAA by defense company Lockheed Martin. It uses satellite-based systems and data communication technologies to improve the efficiency of air traffic controllers. This program is gradually being deployed at en route air traffic control centers.

Other FAA air traffic facilities and government agencies are also connected to the en route centers through ERAM. Among the connected facilities are Terminal Radar Approach Control facilities and towers; the FAA's Command Center in Warrenton, Virginia; automated flight service stations; the Department of Homeland Security; the Department of

Defense; and the US Customs and Border Protection service. ERAM makes it possible for air traffic controllers at each en route air traffic control center to track 1,900 aircraft at a time, 800 more than the original system can handle. The system allows air traffic controllers to coordinate information seamlessly between centers, enabling the use of a 3-mile (4.8 km) separation between planes, rather than the previous 5 miles (8 km). ERAM more efficiently processes flight plan information and automatically transfers information between en route air traffic control centers, even if planes divert from their flight plan. The system also makes air traffic control more efficient in cases of bad weather and congestion. Because the system is satellite-based, it can be used in areas that lack radar coverage.

The FAA is also exploring a move from voice communications to data-based communications between controllers and aircraft. The process works much like text messaging, and the goal is to increase the amount and speed of information transmitted. This change could lead to better routing and fewer delays.

The adoption of new technologies for more efficient routing could lead to less fuel consumption, which means that planes would produce less environmentally harmful carbon emissions. Many other countries are adopting similar advanced systems.

ARTIFICIAL INTELLIGENCE AND BIG DATA

Programming and data analysis have been transformed by artificial intelligence (AI) and machine learning (ML). Artificial intelligence uses software to simulate human intelligence. This process allows computers to make decisions in a way that mimics human thinking. Machine learning is the process by which computers learn from the results of previous decisions, to improve their analytical and decision-making processes. In machine learning, computers are programmed with a set of rules, called algorithms. They use the algorithms to analyze large volumes of data, find the patterns in it, and provide decisions or predictions according to the patterns they find. The results of various decisions are analyzed by computer software, and the best choices are identified. These solutions are ranked, and the best are retained. The analysis and selection processes are then repeated. The computer "learns" more with each iteration. These technologies allow computers to find the patterns in big data—the vast amounts of data collected directly by sensors or stored in databases.

AI and ML have a range of applications in the transportation industry—from transportation system usage data for urban planning to operating autonomous vehicles. Below are some of the applications of AI, ML, and big data in transportation:

Improving public transportation: AI and ML can be used to provide an understanding of customer utilization of various bus, subway, and train routes, including the combinations of these methods used by passengers. This information can be applied to adjust the size, number, and scheduling of existing modes of transportation, as well as to plan for future routes.

Predictive maintenance: By analyzing data collected directly from sensors on components such as brakes, on vehicles, on tracks, and on equipment such as signals, it is possible to use AI and ML to predict when a fault is likely to happen and schedule maintenance before a problem occurs.

Better customer service: AI, ML, and big data can also allow public and private transportation companies to target the correct customers with information on delays, special offers, and new services or changed services.

Faster and more accurate urban planning: Transportation planners need information to design efficient, safe, and sustainable urban transportation systems. Changes in demand from shifting demographics have to be taken into account, such as the increasing numbers of young adults and millennials choosing to live downtown in cities rather than on the outskirts in suburbs. Changes in transportation preferences, such as the use of ride-hailing services like Uber and Lyft rather than taxis or public transportation, must also be considered. Mixed-use housing, which combines apartments, retail stores, and restaurants in one building complex, increases the number of people who walk, bicycle, or use public transportation rather than personal cars. This means that pedestrians, bicycles, and public and private transportation all need to be considered in urban transportation planning. Big data can be collected directly by cameras and sensors on vehicles and roads. The collection of massive mobile data (MMD) allows planners to learn which factors are causing congestion on a specific road—for example, lack of parking causing cars to keep circling, delivery trucks blocking parts of the road, or traffic signals being badly timed. Thus, AI and ML can provide a more efficient analysis of problems and generate more accurate answers.

The fact that computerization and automation are just beginning to be implemented across the transportation system means that there will be a continuing demand for programmers for years to come. Moreover, modernizing transportation systems is just the beginning of the computerization of the transportation industry. The automation of vehicles will radically alter the way people travel and provide significant opportunities for coders.

CHANGING TRANSPORTATION JOBS

Automated tollbooths detect a sensor from cars (called E-ZPass in this photograph) and collect tolls from drivers' accounts.

As automation takes over the transportation field, the number of people holding many traditional transportation jobs will fall significantly. Some jobs will completely disappear. The implementation of smart vehicles will occur first in public transportation and on-demand transportation services. Trains, subways, and buses that can communicate with each other and with control centers will mean fewer personnel to monitor and control these vehicles. Fully automated mass transit vehicles will eliminate the jobs of subway, train, and bus drivers. The number of drivers on trains could also be reduced.

Google is already running a pilot program in Phoenix, Arizona, in which autonomous vans take people to and from the train station. Car service Uber is depending on the development of autonomous cars to solve its problem of driver shortages. Autonomous vehicles don't require pay or benefits, so the availability of autonomous taxis will reduce jobs for human taxi drivers. Similarly, automated trucks are being explored as a means to cope with a shortage of truck drivers, and once the technology is perfected, automated trucks could reduce the jobs available for human drivers. Toll booth operators are already disappearing, replaced by toll booths that automatically read a sensor attached to a car.

New jobs will be created, but they will require technical expertise. Technicians will be needed to install, maintain, and repair autonomous and smart systems, and automated vehicles. Since the smart highway and autonomous vehicle revolution is still in the development stages, coders and programmers are needed to create, test, implement, and modify the computer code used for these applications.

There are all kinds of autonomous vehicles being created. Kiwi is a self-driving autonomous package delivery robot.

chapter_03

New and Innovative Technologies

Computer-controlled equipment, monitoring, and analysis play a major role in today's transportation systems. They will play an even larger role in the future. The number one change in transportation that affects how people travel and how goods are delivered is the development of autonomous vehicles. Already pilot programs using autonomous cars and trucks are being carried out on a limited basis. The types of autonomous vehicles and the applications for them will expand in the future. Computerization is the key to operating autonomous vehicles, for ensuring that they are safe, and for providing security so that they cannot be hacked.

HOW AUTONOMOUS VEHICLES WORK

A number of systems work together to run an autonomous vehicle. Sensors are used to pick up information from the environment and send it to a computer in the vehicle. Radar-based sensors arranged around the vehicle detect the positions of other vehicles. Lidar is a sensor technology that operates much like radar, but instead of bouncing X-rays off objects, it uses light from lasers. Lidar detectors are used on autonomous vehicles to detect the edges of streets and the lane lines on roads. Ultrasonic sensors in the wheels bounce sound waves off objects around the vehicle to detect curbs and other vehicles during parking. Video cameras are used to identify traffic lights, read road signs, and locate other vehicles,

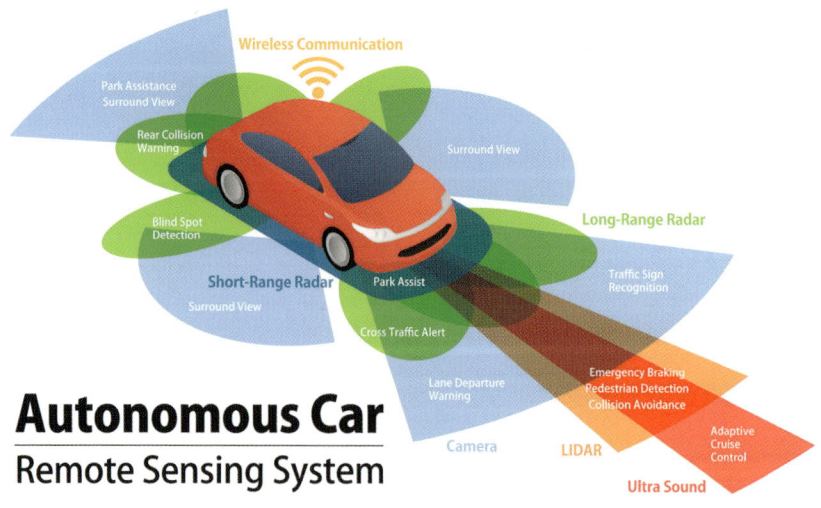

This diagram shows the various sensor systems that pick up information and transmit it to an autonomous vehicle's computer.

pedestrians, and obstacles. The data from these sensors and cameras is sent to a computer in the car. This computer analyzes the data and sends signals to the mechanical systems in the car, adjusting the steering, controlling acceleration, and operating the brakes. Autonomous vehicles, including cars, trucks, trains, planes, and ships, need software programs for sensor data processing, control, security, communication, and data exchange.

PLATOONS OF VEHICLES

One technology being investigated for use with autonomous vehicles is automated driving systems (ADSs). ADSs allow vehicles on a road to communicate with each other, rather than each conveying information only to its own computer. Thus, vehicles with ADSs can operate as one multi-vehicle unit, rather than just as individual vehicles. That can mean more capacity on roads, and faster, more efficient travel. This coordination of multiple vehicles, called platooning, makes it possible to optimize the speed of a group of vehicles, and the distance between them, which allows them to move more efficiently along a road. One trial program designed to demonstrate the feasibility of platooning was carried out at the US Army Aberdeen Proving Ground in Maryland in 2017.

The project used five autonomous Cadillacs and was performed by the Federal Highway Administration's (FHWA)

Turner-Fairbank Highway Research Center (TFHRC), the US Department of Transportation's Volpe National Transportation Systems Center, and the Aberdeen Test Center. The onboard computer of each vehicle was connected to a communication device that allowed vehicle-to-vehicle communication. The cars shared information that enabled them to slow down or speed up in order to stay a specified distance apart. The cars performed successfully.

Programmers were involved in various aspects of the project, including the analytical work and the programming of the onboard computers with platooning algorithms. The FHWA-Volpe Center team is working on an open-source cooperative automated vehicle driving platform.

A platform consists of computer code and tools that can be used to develop applications. Open-source means that the software would be available to any organization that wanted to work on advancing cooperative automated driving technology. The team's goal is to have automotive industry companies partner with them to create automated steering that would allow the "platoon" to change lanes and merge onto highways as a group.

ISSUES WITH AUTONOMOUS VEHICLES

Programmers face a number of issues that must be addressed to ensure acceptance of autonomous vehicles. Manufacturers

This mockup of a platoon of self-driving trucks shows how a real-life platoon could deliver goods more efficiently.

developing autonomous vehicles have promoted several advantages of this technology. Autonomous vehicles are more compliant with the rules of the road and speed limits. They improve safety and save lives by reducing human error, unsafe behavior such as speeding, and driving by compromised drivers. They provide a means of personal transportation for disabled people and those who don't know how to drive.

Public transportation vehicles, such as buses and subway trains, are a natural application for autonomous vehicles because they run on tracks or set routes, which can be well understood by computer navigation programs. However, given the vast number of locations and types of roads on which vehicles operate, there are several issues that need to be addressed in order for general-purpose self-driving vehicles to succeed. Among these are the following:

- Will autonomous vehicles be able to respond to unexpected situations, such as a child running into the street in front of a car, as quickly as a human driver with good reflexes (automatic responses that occur without thought)?

- Can autonomous cars be hacked so that an unauthorized person can remotely take control of a vehicle or disable the computers of a large number of vehicles in transit?

- How will autonomous cars operate in rural or remote areas where roads are not well marked?

- What happens in the event of computer malfunction?

- How well will autonomous cars be able to interact with vehicles driven by human drivers, who often perform unpredictable actions or violate the rules of the road—which autonomous vehicles expect other vehicles to follow?

- Can autonomous cars handle variations in end-of-ride activities, such as going around the back of a building and parking once they reach the coordinates indicating their destination?

- Can they be made to park in a handicap space rather than a regular space? What about pulling up to a pick-up door or loading dock when a consumer needs to pick up merchandise?

The final issue is whether the public will accept autonomous cars. Many—perhaps most—human beings don't trust vehicles they can't control. This is one reason that many people don't like to fly—no matter how many times they are told that flying is safer than driving. In a plane or an autonomous car, they have no control over what happens. In addition, most people have experienced malfunctions and failures with computers and electronic devices. Several studies show that the public does not share the manufacturers' enthusiasm for turning over control of their vehicle to a computer. For example, the 2018 Cox Automotive Evolution of Mobility Study: Autonomous Vehicles found that "consumer awareness of driverless vehicles has skyrocketed and the desire for autonomous features is high;" however, "84 percent want to have the option to drive themselves even in a self-driving vehicle, compared to 16 percent who would feel comfortable letting an autonomous vehicle drive them without the option of being able to take control. The number of respondents that believe roadways would be safer if all vehicles were fully autonomous versus operated by people has decreased 18 percentage points in just two years."

The majority of consumers prefer a vehicle that provides "all the benefits of full vehicle autonomy without stripping away the option of driver control." Forty-nine percent of consumers responded that they would never buy an autonomous-only vehicle (compared to 30 percent in 2016).

HUMAN FACTORS

"Human factors" research is the study of systems that rely on both human beings and machines to operate, such as computers. In the 1980s, human factors expert Earl Wiener came up with Wiener's Laws, fifteen points about human beings relying on computers and automated systems. Here are a few of them, which are still relevant today:

- Every device creates its own opportunity for human error.

- Exotic devices create exotic problems.

- Digital devices tune out small errors while creating opportunities for large errors.

- Whenever you solve a problem you usually create one. You can only hope that the one you created is less critical than the one you eliminated.

Given these points, programmers in the transportation industry are likely to have work for a long time.

Even young survey participants were reluctant to embrace fully autonomous vehicles. Forty-eight percent of twelve to twenty-two year olds, and 39 percent of twenty-three to thirty-six year olds said they would never purchase an autonomous-only vehicle. Similar results have been obtained in other surveys, such as a 2017 survey by the Pew Research Center, and a 2014 survey by the University of Michigan Transportation Research Institute. People are worried that self-driving vehicles may not be safe, may pose security issues, and may not perform as well as human drivers.

SELF-DRIVING TRAINS

The technology by which trains are controlled is changing through computer automation.

Many cities are working on projects to update and automate subway systems. One example is the city of Toronto, Canada, which is planning to replace its existing subway trains with new ones that use automated signaling and can run without a human driver. The target completion date for the project is 2020.

The Toronto Transit Commission's (TTC's) present signaling system divides the track into blocks, each of which has a traffic signal, similar to a traffic light on a road. Signals are monitored by a control center and change to indicate whether a train should proceed along the track or wait. Because there is no way to know exactly where other trains are on the track, train

The TTC streetcar is part of Toronto's mass transit system, which it is automating.

drivers are often instructed to wait a considerable time by the control center. The new system, called communications-based train control (CBTC), uses sensors to allow a train to check its position in relation to other trains automatically. With this system, trains can maintain speed, and more trains can run per hour. CBTC relies on communication devices, called beacons, which are placed on the track. As a train passes over a beacon, it communicates its speed, location, and braking distance to the control center. At the control center, computers process this data and implement real-time adjustments to the train's speed to keep trains safely separated.

The new system will allow the TTC to run thirty-two trains per hour, compared with twenty-five with the current system. More trains mean less crowded transit experiences and shorter wait times. Automatic signaling systems like this one reduce travel time because a train can travel at higher speeds or for more time before braking than with current systems. Improved efficiency also means lower operating costs. More important, such systems eliminate human error and improve safety.

The control of conventional trains is also being automated. Technology company Siemens has created modular smart train control systems that rely on track-to-train communication to enhance safety and operating functions. The automatic train control system Zub 200, which provides a variety of automated functions, is designed to be integrated into existing signaling systems. It continuously monitors speed and braking, and displays the actual speed. If the target speed is exceeded, the system sounds an alarm and automatically applies the brakes. It also provides continuous data to the central control station. More advanced systems, such as the Trainguard LZB 700 M, provide completely automated train operation (ATO), including control of speed and braking, although trains still have a driver present. All of the new automated and smart systems being developed require coders and programmers for applications, from research to software for control, monitoring, and security.

AUTONOMOUS SHIPS

Shipping is a major means of moving cargo. As with other modes of transportation, cost and efficiency are key factors in moving goods. The concept of autonomous ships is just beginning to be explored. The Autonomous Ship Technology Symposium in Amsterdam in 2019 brought together ship designers, fleet owners, naval architects, equipment manufacturers, and maritime research organizations to explore the application of autonomous technology to ships. The areas that must be addressed for autonomous ships to become a reality include the following:

This prototype illustrates Rolls-Royce's vision for autonomous cargo ships.

- **Autonomous navigation technology**

- **Automated onboard systems**

- **E-navigation**

- **Automation software**

- **Maritime remote-control technology**

- **Protection against piracy**

- **Cybersecurity**

Rolls-Royce PLC is leading an autonomous ship project called the Advanced Autonomous Waterborne Applications Initiative (AAWA). The project team is exploring various aspects of creating autonomous ships, including the technological requirements, safety, and legal issues involved. The goal of the project is to create a ship that can sail with a reduced crew by 2020: by 2025, they aim to create a totally unmanned ship operated by remote control; by 2030, to create a remote-controlled, unmanned oceangoing ship; and by 2035, to make a completely autonomous ocean-going vessel.

The creation of new types of vehicles is an exciting prospect. Many developments will occur in the field of transportation over the next decade, and programmers will play key roles in all aspects of it.

This analyst is acquiring data from a vehicle and comparing it to other data.

chapter_04

Programmers in Transportation

In the transportation industry, coders and programmers work in private companies, research facilities, consulting firms, and government agencies. They work in both commercial and research applications. The upgrading of roads and highways and the development of smart and autonomous vehicles are likely to fuel demand for transportation coders and programmers.

TRANSPORTATION ANALYSTS

Transportation analysts use software to perform mathematical analyses that interpret data related to traffic flows, crashes, highway infrastructure, and air quality, among other issues.

They create reports to help both companies and government agencies make decisions about future projects.

Transportation analysts frequently work for a state or federal agency, developing analytical methods and interpreting transportation statistics for a given region. They might perform analyses to evaluate the social, environmental, and economic impact of current and proposed transportation systems, or changes to existing systems. Transportation analysts usually have at least a bachelor's degree in an area related to mathematics or computer programming. Some have a higher degree in transportation engineering or civil engineering.

LOGISTICS DATA ANALYSTS

Logistics data analysts carry out data analyses to establish the best transportation methods and routes for the delivery of goods. They work for individual manufacturing and retail companies, consulting firms, and freight delivery companies. Some work with advanced AI and ML technology in performing their analyses. Transportation analysts usually have at least a bachelor's degree in an area related to mathematics or computer programming. They sometimes go on to obtain a master of business administration (MBA) degree.

The US Bureau of Labor Statistics doesn't break out operations research analysts by industry. However, the bureau predicts that overall demand for operations research analysts will grow 30 percent from 2014 to 2024. Given the changes the transportation industry is undergoing, this is likely to be a healthy job market.

SOFTWARE DEVELOPERS/PROGRAMMERS

Software developers, or programmers, create, test, implement, and modify the programs that run on computers, including those that control and monitor components of smart transportation systems and autonomous vehicles. Programmers usually have at least a bachelor's degree in computer science.

They often work with project managers and company management to establish software project requirements and timelines. Senior programmers might train and supervise junior programmers. In addition to programming skills, programmers must have good organizational skills to design and manage software projects, and good problem-solving skills. They also need good communications skills to explain technical information to nontechnical personnel at the company.

APPLICATIONS PROGRAMMERS

Applications programmers create applications using existing computer software and tools. They work with users at businesses and agencies to establish their requirements for information on subjects related to logistics, tracking usage

software engineer, sensor systems

The antennae-like motion sensor on the wheel of an autonomous vehicle collects data it then sends to the car's computer.

Sensors act as the eyes of self-driving vehicles. A sensor system software engineer provides the software for the sensors used in autonomous vehicles and other smart transportation applications. He or she works with a team of electrical, mechanical, reliability, software, and hardware or vehicle engineers. Sensor systems software engineers design and implement the data and communications programs that allow the sensors embedded into infrastructure and self-driving vehicles to exchange information with the computer. They also analyze data collected from sensor systems, often developing automated tools to collect the data and perform the analysis. They create, test, modify, and upgrade sensor software as required. This job requires at least a bachelor's degree in computer science or a related field, including knowledge of computer languages such as C++ and Python and the methods used to create software for sensors. Familiarity with data analysis and charting tools such as MATLAB, NumPy, or Matplotlib is also necessary.

of transportation, and other elements of transportation. They then develop applications to meet those needs. They provide guides for personnel in how to use the software they develop. They have to create documentation to record the procedures they used to develop the programs, so that this information is available if the application needs to be modified. They also make changes to the applications, as needed. This job requires good communication and problem-solving skills. Applications programmers must have knowledge of commonly used applications software, such as SQL and Oracle, and programming languages used in the transportation and business fields. They sometimes create applications for use in collecting data from locations other than the company or agency's premises—for example, during vehicle operation or at locations on highways. Therefore, they need to be familiar with the programming tools used to make smartphone and web applications.

Most applications programmers have a bachelor's degree in information technology, computer science, management information systems, or another information technology–related field. For some positions, a high school diploma or GED certificate may be acceptable if a job candidate has experience creating applications with commonly used software tools and languages.

Transportation researchers often use notebook computers, which can be taken to different locations. This man is working at NASA's Air Traffic Operations Lab.

AUTONOMOUS VEHICLE PROGRAMMERS

Autonomous vehicle programmers research, create, test, implement, and modify algorithms. They work extensively with robotics, artificial intelligence, and machine learning. They write programs for computers that analyze data from a vehicle's sensors and software in order to operate specific systems such as onboard navigation systems. Autonomous vehicle programmers must develop new ways to achieve artificially intelligent decision-making in uncertain environments. They use machine learning techniques to allow autonomous driving applications to predict and respond to the behavior of traffic.

Autonomous vehicle programmers must have at least a bachelor's degree, and an advanced degree may be required for higher-level positions. They must have knowledge of mathematics related to probability (the likelihood of particular events occurring), artificial intelligence, and machine learning; programming languages such as C++ and Python; robotics (the operation of automated machines); and kinodynamic motion planning (the use of mathematics to solve problems that must take into account the velocity, acceleration, and force of a moving vehicle, together with constraints such as the need to avoid obstacles). They also write programs to run embedded systems, which are systems with a dedicated function within an overall mechanical or electrical system, such as cruise control and anti-lock brakes. Such systems are controlled by a programmable computer chip, called a microprocessor or microcontroller, dedicated to running that specific system.

INTERNSHIPS

An internship is a position offered to students so they can work with industry professionals and learn firsthand what it is like to be a coder. Internships are particularly useful to students who want to work as coders in the transportation field because it gives them a chance to learn the unique characteristics of transportation systems and the features of the new technologies that are being applied to transportation. Internships can be paid or unpaid positions. Some internships are incorporated into computer science or engineering programs at a college or university. In this case, students perform hands-on work in the industry for a semester as part of their education. Other internships are advertised on job search websites or the websites of transportation industry organizations, individual companies, or government agencies. Internship opportunities exist in government and research organizations and in private companies. Interns usually perform basic tasks to assist researchers or programmers in an organization. They might write basic code, compile documentation, or help with the implementation, testing,

This programmer checks software in the back of a self-driving, big-rig truck during a demonstration.

modification, and maintenance of existing and new software applications. Both the US Department of Transportation and many state departments of transportation offer internships for students studying coding.

THE PATHWAYS PROGRAM

The US Department of Transportation offers the Pathways Program, which provides internships for all levels of students. This program provides full- and part-time paid opportunities for students to explore federal careers while still in school. Some students are employed for a set time period up to one year; others continue to be employed beyond one year, as long as needed. Further, some have the chance to transition to a permanent position once they graduate. Students enrolled in high school or GED programs, vocational or technical schools, and undergraduate or graduate college programs are eligible to apply. Intern positions exist at the following agencies, plus several others, all of which are part of the DOT:

- Federal Aviation Administration

- Federal Highway Administration

- Federal Motor Carrier Safety Administration

- Federal Railroad Administration

- Federal Transit Administration

- Maritime Administration

- National Highway Traffic Safety Administration

- Volpe National Transportation Systems Center (Volpe)

For more information on DOT internships, check out the agency's website, https://www.transportation.gov/careers/internships.

WORKFORCE RECRUITMENT PROGRAM FOR COLLEGE STUDENTS WITH DISABILITIES

Another internship program is the Workforce Recruitment Program for College Students with Disabilities (WRP). It connects disabled college students and recent graduates with government agencies by providing both paid summer internships and permanent jobs. The program is cosponsored by the Department of Labor's Office of Disability Employment Policy (ODEP) and the Department of Defense, with the support and participation of many other federal agencies, including the Department of Transportation. Candidates must be US citizens, be enrolled in an academic program at an accredited school, have at least a 3.0 grade point average, and have a certification letter from a state vocational rehabilitation center or the Veterans Administration. More information on the program can be found at http://www.dol.gov/odep/wrp.

In addition to the federal government, many state departments of transportation hire interns to assist in transportation research projects. To find out what internships are available, contact your state's department of transportation or state government job website.

Private companies involved in all aspects of transportation hire interns in programming and data analysis. Companies offering internships include those developing autonomous vehicles, those creating products for smart roads and infrastructure, civil engineering firms involved in highway design, public and private transportation organizations, freight companies such as FedEx and UPS, and a wide range of manufacturing and retail companies that need

WRP and other companies provide internship opportunities for students with disabilities.

logistic analysts and planners to control the distribution of their products.

Internships let students practice their coding skills as part of a team of professionals working in the transportation industry. Participating in an internship allows them to experience the job firsthand and decide whether coding in the transportation industry is the best career choice. Because there are so many different types of projects in the transportation industry, a student might choose to try different internships over the course of his or her academic career. With this approach, students can experience different aspects of the transportation industry and make an informed choice about which area suits them best. Internships also give students valuable experience that can be included on their résumés when they look for a permanent job. This shows potential employers that an applicant is familiar with the technology used in the job. Moreover, interns develop relationships with professionals in the transportation industry, and these contacts can be valuable for referrals or references when they are applying for a permanent job.

CHALLENGES AND ADVANTAGES

One advantage of a coding job in the transportation industry is the chance to work with cutting-edge technology. The industry is changing in a way that radically affects how people move. This field also provides the opportunity to do something that makes it possible for people to travel more efficiently, quickly, and safely. The transportation industry provides a variety of options for jobs. One can work for private companies developing new technology, in large public transportation organizations, or at government agencies doing transportation research. Coders in the transportation industry usually receive good salaries and benefits. Programming in the transportation industry provides great job security as well.

Disadvantages of a coding career include having to work long hours when information or a program is needed by a deadline. Coding projects in the transportation industry are performed by teams, so programmers must be able to work well with others, which means adapting to others' working styles and personalities, and being able to compromise when there is a disagreement. This is a field in which formal education is a necessity. Because transportation involves both machine operation and infrastructure, coders need to understand more than computer languages. They need to have a basic knowledge of the engineering principles involved in transportation. Those who will obtain the best jobs need to understand how to code for artificial intelligence, machine learning, and robotics. Therefore, one must be willing to commit oneself to learning math and computer science. However, the rewards can be substantial, both financially and in job satisfaction, for those willing to put in the effort.

Students in a computer lab gain hands-on experience with programming.

chapter_05

Preparing for a Coding Career

To succeed as a coder in the transportation industry, programmers need both technical and personal skills. To obtain a coding job in the transportation industry, you will need to learn computer languages such as Python as well as machine learning and artificial intelligence techniques. During your first job, and in the course of your career, you might work on a variety of applications. You might have to create software that analyzes data from sensors or design a program for a control system for an autonomous vehicle. You might work on applications that look for patterns in traffic data stored in databases or acquired in real time from sensors in the field. Therefore, you will enhance your job prospects if you develop a broad range of skills, including various computer languages, applications, and statistical techniques.

HIGH SCHOOL PREPARATION

Coders in the transportation industry will often work on programs designed to control transportation systems as well as conventional and autonomous vehicles. Therefore, they need to understand the principles of math and physics involved in the operation of both vehicles and electrical systems such as traffic lights and sensors. The foundation for creating computer algorithms and analyzing data is mathematics. Studying math and physics in high school provides the basic knowledge necessary to learn computer science and engineering principles in college.

To create computer algorithms, one must understand a branch of mathematics called calculus. To gain a solid foundation in mathematics and prepare for courses in advanced mathematics in college, you should take classes in algebra and precalculus in high school. (If a class in calculus is available in your school, you should take that as well.) It is also important to understand probability and statistics. Statistics is used both in the analysis of data and in the programming of autonomous vehicles.

In a transportation programming job, you will work as part of a team. However, your interactions with others will not be limited to your fellow programmers. You will have to communicate effectively—both verbally and in writing—with engineers, manufacturing personnel, business managers, and other nonprogrammers. You will need to be able to explain the technical aspects of computer applications to nonprogrammers clearly and in a way that they understand. You will write documentation for the software you create and reports about the results of data you analyze. Thus, you must learn to organize your ideas and speak and write in a clear way. To communicate effectively, you need to understand and use correct English grammar and syntax. Proper grammar and syntax make your meaning clear, minimizing ambiguity and confusion, and also make you appear more professional. If it is possible to take a course in public speaking at your school, doing so can help you learn to communicate effectively. Coders spend the bulk of their time at a keyboard. Taking a typing or keyboarding course can make you more efficient.

DEVELOPING YOUR SKILLS

Gaining coding experience in high school can benefit you in several ways. First, it gives you practice in using a computer language and an understanding of how to create computer algorithms. This knowledge will make it easier for you to learn other computer languages and more advanced techniques in college and on the job. Moreover, it gives you the opportunity to learn if you like coding and want to pursue it as a career,

A high school student assembles a simple robot—an excellent way to learn about robotics.

as well as a chance to identify skills you need to work on. If your high school offers a course in computers or has a computer club in which students create software, these are excellent places to learn more about coding and test your skills. Companies such as Apple and Microsoft offer development kits for those interested in making apps. You can share your apps with friends, post them on social media, or even sell them through a site such as Apple's App Store or Google's Play Store. Having a portfolio of apps can also be useful when applying for a job. If you want to learn a computer language such as Python or C++ while in high school, there are books, CDs, and online courses that offer training in specific languages. If you want to learn more about the mechanical and electrical aspects of robotics, there are online tutorials as well as books with do-it-yourself projects that allow you to create various types of simple robots and learn the techniques involved.

Another way to learn about programming tools and issues is to join a professional organization. There are computing industry organizations that can aid in your development. Two of the largest such organizations are the Association for Computing Machinery (ACM) and the Institute of Electrical and Electronics Engineers (IEEE). These organizations provide standards and information for computing in the transportation industry, among others. They both provide special resources and memberships for students.

EDUCATION FOR CODING

Most programming jobs require a four-year college degree in computer science or a related field. In some cases, experienced programmers are hired with an associate's degree or even just a high school diploma or GED, but the environment for entry-level jobs is competitive. In most cases, candidates who are hired without a bachelor's degree have at least two years of hands-on coding experience or have taken nondegree courses in programming. For those interested in higher-level jobs, a master's degree is desirable. Many colleges and universities offer four-year bachelor's degrees as well as master's and PhD degrees. Technical institutes provide both four-year degree programs and two-year associate's

AUTONOMOUS DRIVING INTERNS

Autonomous driving interns, like these General Motors engineering interns, assist in the development of software for self-driving vehicles.

Autonomous driving interns have the opportunity to learn about developing autonomous driving applications by assisting in the development of software programs and embedded hardware applications. They use computer science methods and techniques to store, manipulate, transform, or present information using computer systems. This position requires only a high school diploma, but these programmers must have a working knowledge of computer systems, mathematics used in computer systems—such as linear algebra, trigonometry, calculus, probability, and statistics—and computer languages such as C++, Java, and Linux. To work with automotive mechanical and electrical systems, it is necessary to have knowledge of basic physics and electrical circuits. Interns are supervised by a senior-level programmer. An autonomous driving intern helps solve complex technical challenges in areas like robotics, perception, decision-making, and deep learning, while collaborating with hardware and systems engineers. The intern researches and helps develop cutting-edge ML techniques for self-driving cars, and big data analysis tools to make sense of large amounts of data. He or she also tests new systems and assists in improving existing ones.

degrees. Students can also obtain a degree online. However, if you decide to pursue a degree online, make sure to check the US Department of Education database of accredited colleges (https://ope.ed.gov/dapip/#/home). This ensures that you can obtain a valid degree and that you can transfer credits to another school, if necessary.

Programming students begin by taking general courses in computer science, such as introduction to computer systems, courses in specific computer languages, and computational mathematics. Students also take a variety of elective courses in computer science in specific areas that interest them. For those interested in coding for the transportation industry, such course choices might include robotics, which covers the automating of machines; artificial intelligence and machine learning; data mining; and possibly cybersecurity. Students will also take mathematics courses, including advanced calculus and algebra, statistics, and probability, which analyzes the likelihood of various events occurring. For working with transportation systems, an understanding of engineering and physics principles is important, so it is advisable to take courses in physics and engineering, as well as experimental design.

Some colleges offer courses in automation or sensors and signaling processes, which can enhance one's knowledge of the field. Another course that can be helpful is one in human factors, the study of how people respond to interaction with machines such as autonomous vehicles. Knowledge of this area of study can help you design features that are better accepted by users. Your school might also require computer science students to take a course in ethical computing. This course explains how to treat people's data in a way that protects their privacy and confidentiality.

Students should also take humanities and arts courses. Among the courses that can be helpful in designing transportation applications and working with others on the job are psychology and the literatures, histories, and languages of other cultures. In the workplace you will participate on teams with people from diverse cultures, so it can be valuable to have an understanding of other people's history and culture. In addition, transportation systems and autonomous vehicles are used by people with different backgrounds and language skills, so these types of courses can help you better design applications for users. Learning a foreign language is desirable as well because working on transportation projects often involves travel to other countries to work on joint projects, study others' transportation projects, or share information at conferences.

CONTINUING EDUCATION

A coder's education never ends, especially in an industry that is changing as rapidly as transportation. It is imperative that a programmer stays current with new computer languages, applications, and devices as they are developed. Programmers can learn new software and hardware technologies through courses, books, online tutorials, and participation in professional organizations. Many computer professionals begin their careers with a bachelor's degree and then go on to pursue a master's degree in computer science, robotics, or engineering.

The transportation industry has changed greatly over the years. In the twenty-first century, this evolution is continuing, and many intriguing changes are occurring. The computerization of transportation systems and the development of new types of vehicles are creating jobs for programmers who want to work with cutting-edge technology. Such careers and technological advances will transform the way people and goods travel, and benefit society as a whole.

A diverse team of programmers works on code during the Google I/O Developers Conference in 2018.

Glossary

acquire In terms of computers, to collect data.

artificial intelligence (AI) The programming of computers to learn and make decisions in a manner similar to the way that human beings do.

automate To use computer technology to allow a vehicle or system to control itself.

autonomous Describes a device or vehicle that runs by itself without human control.

big data Vast amounts of information captured from databases and direct sources such as sensors.

cartel A group of countries or companies in an industry that jointly manages that industry.

convey To communicate information.

cybersecurity The process of protecting computers and data.

divert To switch from one direction to another.

drone A remotely controlled unmanned vehicle; most often a type of aircraft.

hack To break into a computer system.

infrastructure The basic facilities and systems necessary for the transportation, or other operations, within a city, state, or country.

internal combustion A process by which gasoline or other fuel mixed with oxygen is burned to generate energy to power an engine.

iteration A repetition of a series of steps.

kinodynamic motion planning The use of mathematics to solve problems related to the velocity, acceleration, and force of a moving vehicle.

logistics The planning and control for moving goods or people from one place to another.

machine learning (ML) A process by which software is used to allow a computer to improve its responses based on the success of its previous decisions.

maritime Related to the sea.

millennials People who reached young adulthood in the early twenty-first century.

mimic To copy.

mixed-use housing Building complexes that contain both apartments and commercial enterprises such as retail stores and restaurants in one building complex.

nautical mile An international standard of measurement equal to 6,076 feet (564 meters).

optimize To perform in the most efficient and effective way.

predictive maintenance Using computer software to forecast when maintenance on a component is likely to be required.

sensor An electronic device that is placed on a component; it detects specific objects or conditions and sends information to a computer.

syntax The rules that govern usage in a human or computer language.

FURTHER INFORMATION

BOOKS

Bedell, Jane. *So You Want to Be a Coder?* New York: Aladdin/ Beyond Words, 2016.

Gerrish, Sean. *How Smart Machines Think.* Cambridge, MA: MIT Press, 2018.

McPherson, Stephanie Sammartino. *Artificial Intelligence: Building Smarter Machines.* Minneapolis, MN: Lerner/Twenty-First Century Books, 2018.

Xiang, David. *Software Developer Life: Career, Learning, Coding, Daily Life, Stories.* Self-published, Amazon Digital Services, 2018.

WEBSITES
DREAM IN CODE
http://www.dreamincode.net/forums/
forum/78-programming-tutorials
This website provides links to online tutorials for a variety of computer languages for students who want to learn them.

GIRL DEVELOP IT
http://www.girldevelopit.com
This website gives information about software development classes and how girls, specifically, can get involved.

ORGANIZATIONS

ASSOCIATION FOR COMPUTING MACHINERY (ACM)

https://www.acm.org

ACM is a major organization for professionals in the computing industry. It provides a number of resources, including publications specifically for students.

INSTITUTE OF ELECTRICAL AND ELECTRONICS ENGINEERS (IEEE)

https://www.ieee.org

The premiere professional organization for the electronics and electrical engineering professions, IEEE maintains a student portal on its website for young people interested in technology careers and provides a number of special programs for them.

US DEPARTMENT OF TRANSPORTATION (DOT)

https://www.transportation.gov

The DOT provides information on the transportation field, performs research, and supports students through internships for young people interested in pursuing a career in the transportation industry.

Selected Bibliography

"Automatic Train Control Systems." Siemens. Accessed December 27, 2018. https://www.mobility.siemens.com/mobility/global/en/urban-mobility/rail-solutions/rail-automation/automatic-train-control-system/pages/automatic-train-control-system.aspx.

Bharadwaj, Raghav. "AI in Transportation–Current and Future Business-Use Applications." Emerj, December 12, 2018. https://emerj.com/ai-sector-overviews/ai-in-transportation-current-and-future-business-use-applications.

Clifford, Tori. "5 Urban Transportation Challenges that Big Data Can Help You Solve." Streetlight Data, March 30, 2017. https://www.streetlightdata.com/5-urban-transportation-challenges-that-big-data-can-help-you-solve.

"Computer Chips Inside the Car." Chips Etc. Accessed December 29, 2018. http://www.chipsetc.com/computer-chips-inside-the-car.html.

"Fact Sheet–En Route Automation Modernization (ERAM)." Federal Aviation Administration, April 29, 2015. https://www.faa.gov/news/fact_sheets/news_story.cfm?newsId=7714.

Gerage, Alex. "Three Ways Machine Learning Will Disrupt Transportation." Northwestern McCormick School of

Engineering. October 27, 2016. https://www.mccormick.
northwestern.edu/news/articles/2016/10/three-ways-
machine-learning-will-disrupt-transportation.html.

"History of the Automobile." Encyclopedia Britannica. Accessed
December 29, 2018. https://www.britannica.com/technology/
automobile/History-of-the-automobile.

"How An Automated Car Platoon Works." US Department of
Transportation Volpe National Transportation Systems Center.
Accessed January 3, 2019. https://www.transportation.gov/
connections/how-automated-car-platoon-works.

Kochhar, Dushiant. "Big Data in Public Transportation." Hortonworks,
June 1, 2016. https://hortonworks.com/blog/big-data-public-
transportation.

Kulkarni, Nitish. "Air Traffic Control Is Getting A Much-Needed
Upgrade." TechCrunch. Accessed December 27, 2018. https://
techcrunch.com/2015/08/16/air-traffic-control-is-getting-a-
much-needed-upgrade.

Lipson, Hod, and Melba Kurman. *Driverless: Intelligent Cars and the
Road Ahead.* Cambridge, MA: MIT Press, 2017.

"Mapping and Geographic Information Systems (GIS): What Is
GIS?" University of Wisconsin—Madison Libraries. Accessed
November 7, 2018. https://researchguides.library.wisc.edu/GIS.

Rolls-Royce PLC. *Autonomous Ships: The Next Step*. Rolls-Royce PLC, 2016. https://www.rolls-royce.com/~/media/Files/R/Rolls-Royce/documents/customers/marine/ship-intel/rr-ship-intel-aawa-8pg.pdf.

Simoudis, Evangelos. *The Big Data Opportunity in Our Driverless Future*. Menlo Park, CA: Corporate Innovators LLC, 2017.

"SURTRAC: Real-Time Adaptive Traffic Signal Control." Rapid Flow. Accessed January 1, 2019. https://www.rapidflowtech.com.

"TTC Automated Train Control Soon to Be a Reality." George Brown College, April 16, 2018. https://www.automationprogram.com/ttc-automated-train-control-soon-to-be-a-reality.php.

US Department of Transportation. *Research, Development, and Technology Strategic Plan FY2017–2021*. December 2016. https://www.transportation.gov/sites/dot.gov/files/docs/USDOT-RD%26T-Strategic-Plan-Final-011117.pdf.

Weisfeld, Matt. "What Skills Employers Want in a Software Developer: My Conversations with Companies Who Hire Programmers." InformIt/Pearson, November 12, 2013. http://www.informit.com/articles/article.aspx?p=2156240.

INDEX

ABOUT THE AUTHOR

Jeri Freedman has a bachelor of arts degree from Harvard University. For fifteen years she worked for high-technology companies involved in cutting-edge technologies, including advanced semiconductors and scientific testing equipment. She was the cofounder of Innovative Applications, a small computer company selling and customizing accounting software. She is the author of more than fifty young adult nonfiction books, including *Digital Career Building Through Skinning and Modding*, *Careers in Computer Support*, *High-Tech Jobs: Software Development*, and *Cyber Citizenship and Cyber Safety: Intellectual Property*.